HARD AS NAILS
Kings and Queens

TRACEY TURNER
ILLUSTRATED BY JAMIE LENMAN

Crabtree Publishing Company
www.crabtreebooks.com

Crabtree Publishing Company
www.crabtreebooks.com
1-800-387-7650

616 Welland Ave.
St. Catharines, ON
L2M 5V6

PMB 59051, 350 Fifth Ave.
59th Floor,
New York, NY

Published by Crabtree Publishing Company in 2016.

Author: Tracey Turner

Illustrator: Jamie Lenman

Project coordinator: Kelly Spence

Editor: Becca Sjonger

Proofreader: Wendy Scavuzzo

Prepress technician: Tammy McGarr

Print coordinator: Margaret Amy Salter

Copyright © 2015 A & C Black

Text copyright © 2015 Tracey Turner

Illustrations copyright © 2015 Jamie Lenman

Additional illustrations © Shutterstock

First published 2015 by
A & C Black, an imprint of
Bloomsbury Publishing Plc.

Printed in the USA/082015/SN20150529

Library and Archives Canada
Cataloguing in Publication

Turner, Tracey, author
        Hard as nails kings and queens / Tracey
Turner ; Jamie Lenman, illustrator.

(Hard as nails in history)
Includes index.
ISBN 978-0-7787-1519-1 (bound).--ISBN 978-0-
7787-1523-8 (paperback)

        1. Kings and rulers--Biography--Juvenile
literature. 2. Queens--Biography--Juvenile
literature. 3. Kings and rulers--Juvenile literature.
4. Queens--Juvenile literature. 5. Royal houses-
-Juvenile literature. 6. Monarchy--Juvenile
literature. I. Lenman, Jamie, illustrator II. Title.

D106.T87 2015   j321.0092'2   C2015-903042-0

Library of Congress
Cataloging-in-Publication Data

Turner, Tracey.
 Hard as nails kings and queens / Tracey Turner ;
illustrated by Jamie Lenman.
        pages cm. -- (Hard as nails in history)
 Includes index.
 ISBN 978-0-7787-1519-1 (reinforced library
binding : alk. paper) -- ISBN 978-0-7787-1523-8
(pbk. : alk. paper)
1. Kings and rulers--Juvenile literature. 2.
Queens--Juvenile literature. 3. World history--
Juvenile literature. I. Lenman, Jamie, illustrator.
II. Title.

JC375.T87 2015
321.0092'2--dc23
                                                                2015014837

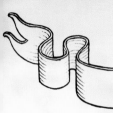

CONTENTS

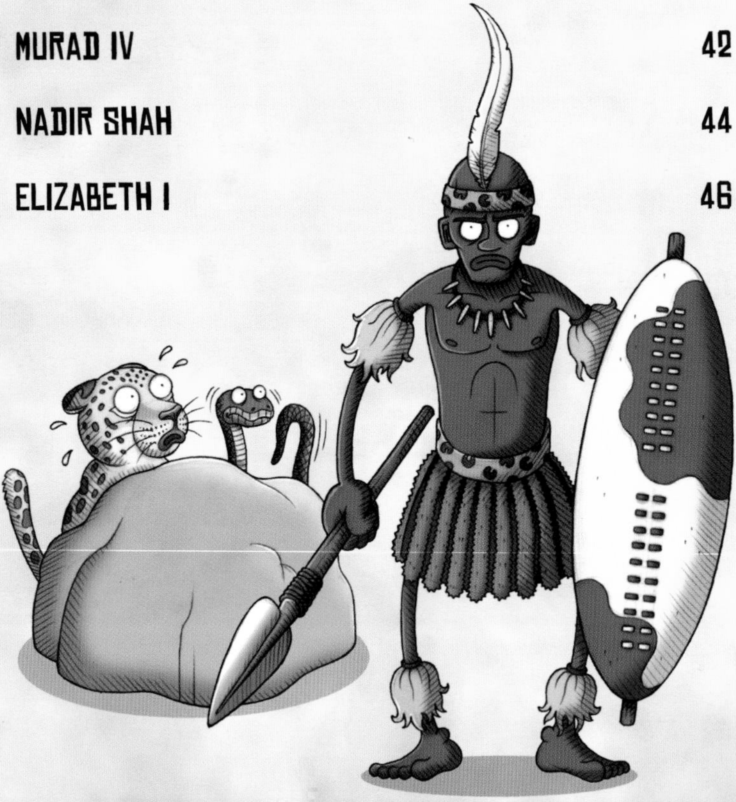

INTRODUCTION

This book contains some of the toughest kings and queens ever, from terrifying czars to savage sultans. Some of them were power-crazed tyrants, some were ax-wielding warriors, and some were oddballs. But all of them were as hard as nails.

FIND OUT ABOUT . . .

- Horrible human sacrifice

- Brave runaway slaves

- Tremendous elephant-mounted armies

- Head-chopping, eye-gouging, and burning at the stake

If you've ever wanted to be worshiped by millions, command a Persian fleet, or become empress of China, read on. Follow the royals through the plains of central India, into the Aztec capital city, and across the Pacific Ocean by canoe.

As well as discovering stories of courage and cunning, you might be in for a few surprises. Did you know that King Henry VIII had more than 50,000 people's heads chopped off? Or that Thutmose III tried to have his predecessor's name deleted from history?

You're about to meet some of the toughest kings and queens in history . . .

Plus take the quiz on page 28 to find out how well you know monarch's nicknames!

QUEEN ARTEMISIA

Queen Artemisia was a brave and clever sea commander in the Persian War with Greece.

PERSIAN OVERLORDS

Artemisia was queen of Halicarnassus, which was part of the massive and mighty Persian Empire. She was a fierce warrior queen who nearly changed the course of history.

COUNCIL OF WAR

The powerful Persian Emperor Xerxes I wanted to expand his empire into Greece. He had already made one unsuccessful attempt at grabbing Greece before he turned to Artemisia and the other commanders of the Persian fleet in 480 BCE. Artemisia was unusual among the Persian commanders in two ways. First, she was a woman. Second, she was the only commander who advised Xerxes against his planned sea battle. She thought it was too risky, and it would be better to wait. Xerxes listened and praised Artemisia for her wise advice. Then he completely ignored it and gave the order to set sail.

THE BATTLE OF SALAMIS

HARDOMETER

CUNNING: 8
COURAGE: 9
SURVIVAL SKILLS: 8
RUTHLESSNESS: 8

Artemisia was in command of five ships at the Battle of Salamis. She fought bravely and with ruthless cunning, sometimes flying the Greek flag to confuse her enemies. At one point in the battle, a Persian ship blocked her escape route. She rammed the ship and sank it to get away. Xerxes didn't seem to mind, though. He thought Artemisia was his best commander. Xerves reportedly said, "My men have become women and my women men," (which was the way a lot of people thought in those days). However, despite Artemisia's best efforts, the Persians were defeated by the Greeks.

THE PERSIANS GO HOME

Xerxes consulted his commanders on whether he should leave some of the Persian fleet in Greece. This time, he listened to Artemisia and they all went home. If he had taken her advice in the first place, maybe the Persians would have conquered Greece and changed the course of history. The Greeks, meanwhile, were very happy they had won. But they were furious that a woman had commanded ships in a battle against their fleet. They offered a reward for Artemisia's capture, but no one ever succeeded.

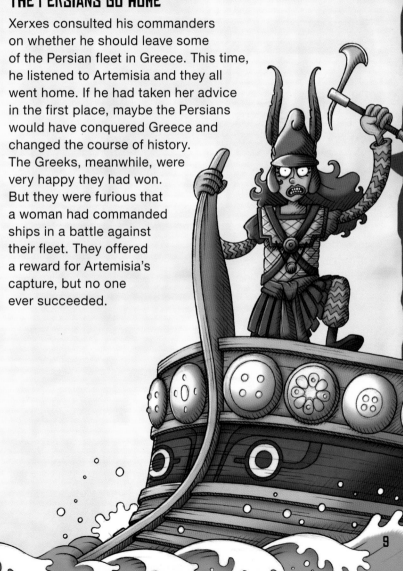

HENRY VIII

Henry VIII is probably the best-known English king. He is famous for having six wives and for plenty of head-chopping.

HANDSOME HENRY

Henry wasn't supposed to be king at all, but became heir to the throne when his older brother died. He was a tall, strong 18-year-old when he became king in 1509. He was smart, musical, good at archery and riding horses, and very popular, despite waging an expensive war against France. (To keep the French at bay, Henry increased the size of the navy ten times, including adding the world's biggest ship.)

UPSETTING THE POPE

Henry was married to the Spanish princess Catherine of Aragon for nearly 24 years. They had a daughter, but Henry desperately wanted a son who would become king after him. So he divorced Catherine and married Anne Boleyn. As a result, the Pope threw him out of the Roman Catholic Church, because divorce wasn't allowed. Henry then set up the Church of England, with himself as its head. This gave him a great excuse to get rid of 800 monasteries and sell off their land and wealth.

SEVERAL MORE WIVES

Anne Boleyn was the second of Henry's six wives. He had her beheaded, and the same fate was in store for his fifth wife, Catherine Howard. In between, there was Jane Seymour, who died soon after producing a son for Henry, and Anne of Cleves, who Henry divorced because he thought she wasn't as nice-looking as the portrait he had seen of her before they met. Henry's sixth wife, Catherine Parr, outlived him.

OFF WITH HIS HEAD!

Wives weren't the only people Henry had executed. Henry set a record for beheadings. No one's quite sure how many people were executed during Henry's reign, but it was probably somewhere between 57,000 and 72,000. Henry became more and more ruthless as he got older. He had a growing habit of executing men who had once been close friends and advisers.

AFTER HENRY

In his last years, Henry became very fat and ill. He had painful ulcers on his legs that made it difficult for him to move. When he died in 1547, his nine-year-old son became Edward VI, but he died six years later. Both of Henry's daughters, Mary and Elizabeth (see page 46), became queens after that.

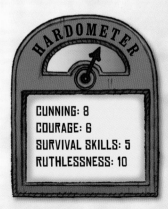

HARDOMETER

CUNNING: 8
COURAGE: 6
SURVIVAL SKILLS: 5
RUTHLESSNESS: 10

FERDINAND II AND ISABELLA I

**HARD AS NAILS
RATING: 7.8**

Ferdinand and Isabella were the first king and queen of a united Spain. They were known as the Catholic Monarchs because they were so focused on their religion.

UNITED SPAIN

Isabella was queen of Castile when she married Ferdinand, the king of Aragon. Although the two large Spanish kingdoms were ruled separately at first, they were later united. Before the end of their reign, all of Spain would be ruled as one kingdom.

RELIGIOUS ROYALS

Ferdinand and Isabella were Catholics, and they were fed up with people from other religions starting rebellions. So they kicked all the Jewish and Muslim people out of Spain, unless they converted to Christianity. But then the king and queen began to accuse people who had converted to Christianity of going back to their old religions. They imprisoned, interrogated, tortured, and even burned to death hundreds of people.

HARDOMETER

CUNNING: 7
COURAGE: 6
SURVIVAL SKILLS: 9
RUTHLESSNESS: 9

GRABBING GRANADA

The Catholic Monarchs were very annoyed that a large chunk of Spain was ruled by Muslims—invaders from North Africa, known as Moors. They had ruled most of Spain for hundreds of years. When Ferdinand and

Isabella were in charge, the Moors ruled the Kingdom of Granada. But Ferdinand and Isabella put a stop to that. After ten years of fighting, the Moors were finally defeated at the city of Granada in 1492.

NEW WORLD RICHES

Once they had dealt with the Moors and the other non-Christians, Ferdinand and Isabella could concentrate on other things—such as discovering the New World. In 1492, they funded Christopher Columbus's expedition to find a sea route to India by sailing west. The new lands he discovered were claimed for Spain (without asking the people who already lived there), and Spain became richer as a result.

MARRIAGES AND AGREEMENTS

Ferdinand and Isabella wanted to protect their united country. They signed agreements with England and the Holy Roman Empire. They also married off some of their children (including Catherine of Aragon, who married Henry VIII—see page 10) to royal families in Europe who supported them. Isabella died in 1504, and Ferdinand died 12 years later. Spain has remained united ever since.

ASHURNASIRPAL II

Ashurnasirpal was a conquering king who made Assyria wealthy and powerful.

HARD TIMES

Ashurnasirpal became king of Assyria (now part of Iraq) in 883 BCE. Assyria had been a powerful country in the past. However, by Ashurnasirpal's time things weren't going so well, and the country had lost some of its land. Ashurnasirpal had plans to make Assyria—and himself—much richer and more powerful.

CRUEL CONQUEROR

Ashurnasirpal marched his army to the north and east of Assyria in a series of attacks against neighboring lands. He made local rulers send him money and gifts, and accept him as their ruler. He was ruthless when anyone opposed him. He had governors publicly whipped, burned many of the prisoners he captured, and blinded enemy soldiers or cut off their hands, noses, or ears. At least, he boasted about those things in his own inscriptions in his new capital city.

CAPITAL CITY

Ashurnasirpal used the loot and the prisoners of war to build an extremely impressive new capital city at Kalhu (modern-day Nimrud in Iraq). Kalhu included a luxurious palace, and zoological and botanical gardens. Canals were built from the Great Zab River to water them. The palace was huge. An inscription at the palace mentions a massive banquet for 69,574 guests that lasted ten days. It celebrated the opening of the rebuilt city in 879 BCE. He also built fortresses on the Tigris and Euphrates rivers,

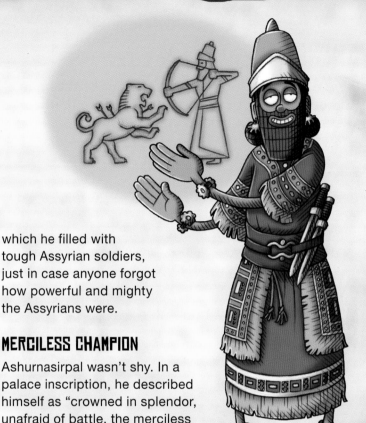

which he filled with tough Assyrian soldiers, just in case anyone forgot how powerful and mighty the Assyrians were.

MERCILESS CHAMPION

Ashurnasirpal wasn't shy. In a palace inscription, he described himself as "crowned in splendor, unafraid of battle, the merciless champion who shakes resistance, the glorious king, the shepherd, the protector of the whole world . . ." He also claimed to have personally killed 450 lions. When Ashurnasirpal died in 859 BCE, he had conquered most of the land that had been lost for centuries.In the 24 years he was king, Ashurnasirpal established a new Assyrian Empire.

HARDOMETER

CUNNING: 8
COURAGE: 6
SURVIVAL SKILLS: 8
RUTHLESSNESS: 10

ANCIENT EMPIRES

Most of us have heard of the ancient Greeks and Romans. But thousands of years before them, cities were built, civilizations flourished, and empires were created . . .

MESOPOTAMIA

The world's first cities were built in Sumer, southern Mesopotamia (modern-day Iraq), in the fertile land between the Tigris and Euphrates rivers. Uruk, considered the world's first city, was built around 6,500 years ago. Many empires came and went in Mesopotamia:

- Sargon, the world's first emperor, ruled the Akkadian Empire in Sumer in around 2300 BCE.

- Babylonia had the world's first written laws. Its capital, Babylon, was built around 1900 BCE and later had famous gardens.

- The fierce Hittites, who came from what is now southern Turkey, crushed the Babylonians and destroyed Babylon . . .

- . . . then the Assyrians, expert charioteers, conquered the Hittites in the eighth century BCE.

- The Babylonians (called the New Babylonians by historians to avoid confusion) defeated the Assyrians in 608 BCE. They could predict eclipses of the moon.

- Finally, the Persian Empire, started by King Cyrus, covered all the land of the earlier Mesopotamian empires. It was the biggest empire in the world up to that time.

ANCIENT EGYPT

Egypt was the world's first country.
Upper and Lower Egypt were united
by King Narmer around 3200 BCE.
It lasted for almost 3,000 years, until it
became part of Alexander the Great's
empire in 332 BCE. After that, it was
ruled by non-Egyptian pharaohs (the
first one was Alexander the Great's
general, Ptolemy).

ANCIENT CHINA

The first cities were built in the Yellow
River valley in China around 1600 BCE.
The first Chinese emperor, Shihuangdi,
united the states of China in 206 BCE.
After Shihuangdi's Qin dynasty, China
was ruled by a series of dynasties
until the twentieth century.

ANCIENT INDIA

The first civilization in the Indus Valley
is mysterious—it was only discovered
150 years ago, and no one knows
much about it. Cities, such as
Mohenjo-Daro, were built more
than 4,000 years ago. They had
roads, sewers, and even toilets,
but no huge palaces or temples.
Its written language is still waiting
to be deciphered.

17

HARALD HARDRADA

Viking King Harald's nickname, Hardrada, means "hard ruler," and it's not difficult to see how he got it.

HARD AS NAILS RATING: 7

FIERCE FIGHTER

Harald's brother wanted to get his hands on the Danish throne. So Harald fought in his first big battle when he was just 15, against the Danish King Cnut. Harald was wounded and lost the battle, but it didn't stop him from fighting. First, he joined the army of Yaroslav the Wise in Russia. Then he moved on to Constantinople, where he commanded a tough, ax-wielding unit of the Byzantine army, and grew very rich at the same time.

KING OF NORWAY

Harald left Constantinople because he had his eye on the throne of Norway. It was occupied by his nephew, Magnus the Good. Harald persuaded Magnus to become joint king with him, and share Harald's massive wealth. Conveniently, Magnus died the following year. To make sure he stayed king, Harald crushed opposition to his rule and had political opponents assassinated.

Then he began making raids on the Danish coast and fought the Danish king in an attempt to become king of Denmark, too. In the end, he gave up.

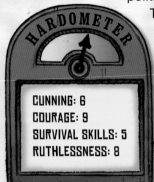

CUNNING: 6
COURAGE: 9
SURVIVAL SKILLS: 5
RUTHLESSNESS: 8

HARALD VS. HAROLD

The king of England was Harold Godwinson. Godwinson's brother, Tostig, suggested to Harald Hardrada that he might want to become the king of England instead, with Tostig's help. After a revolt, Harald had taken Tostig's title of Earl of Northumbria instead of sticking up for his brother. Harald didn't need to be asked twice. He landed on the coast of northern England in 1066 with 300 ships, and defeated English troops at the Battle of Fulford. He captured York, and things seemed to be going well for him.

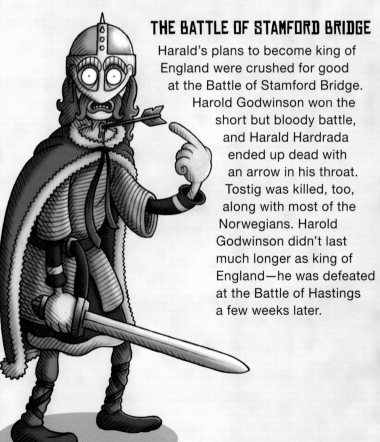

THE BATTLE OF STAMFORD BRIDGE

Harald's plans to become king of England were crushed for good at the Battle of Stamford Bridge. Harold Godwinson won the short but bloody battle, and Harald Hardrada ended up dead with an arrow in his throat. Tostig was killed, too, along with most of the Norwegians. Harold Godwinson didn't last much longer as king of England—he was defeated at the Battle of Hastings a few weeks later.

NZINGA MBANDE

**Nzinga Mbande was an
African queen who set up
an army camp for runaway slaves
and successfully defended her kingdom.**

PORTUGUESE INVADERS

At the beginning of the 1600s, African states on the central
African coast were threatened by the Portuguese. They
wanted to take charge of the region and control the trade
of African slaves, who were shipped across the Atlantic
to the New World. The Portuguese governor of Luanda
(today the capital of Angola), went to war with the Kingdom
of Ndongo. King Ngola Mbandi of the Ndongo ran away,
leaving his tough sister, Nzinga, to rule. Thousands of
Ndongo people became prisoners of the Portuguese.

NZINGA IN CHARGE

There are many different versions of Nzinga's story.
Some say that her brother killed himself, while others
say that Nzinga killed him so that she could seize power.
But whatever happened, Nzinga ended up in charge
in 1624. She made an agreement with the Portuguese
that they would return the Ndongo
prisoners, and remove the fortress
they had built on Ndongo land.
Within a couple of years, she
was betrayed.

CUNNING: 8
COURAGE: 8
SURVIVAL SKILLS: 9
RUTHLESSNESS: 5

LEAVING NDONGO

Nzinga and her people fled west and founded a new state at Matamba. Nzinga set up a military school, and invited runaway slaves and African soldiers trained by the Portuguese to join. She also stirred up trouble in Ndongo, which was then controlled by the Portuguese.

DUTCH FRIENDS

The Dutch also wanted to get rid of the Portuguese, and Nzinga became their ally. At one point, the Dutch captured Luanda. Even with Nzinga's help, they couldn't drive out the Portuguese completely, and Luanda was recaptured. Nzinga retreated to Matamba again, and focused on looking after her land, protecting it from the Portuguese, and making it rich. She was still fighting against the Portuguese into her sixties.

OLD ENEMIES

Nzinga achieved her goals. By the time she died of old age when she was 81, she had also gained the respect of her enemies. Matamba was able to trade on an equal footing with the Europeans.

CHANDRAGUPTA

Chandragupta conquered vast chunks of India, and began the massive Mauryan Empire.

DIVIDED INDIA

When Chandragupta was born in 340 BCE, India wasn't a united country but was made up of different independent states. The biggest was the Magadha kingdom in northern India, ruled by the Nanda dynasty. Another large chunk of northern India had been defeated by Alexander the Great in 326 BCE and became part of the Macedonian Empire.

THROWING OUT THE NANDAS

Chandragupta was related to the Nandas, but he lived in exile. He decided to kick out the Macedonians and the Nanda dynasty, and make a new empire himself. With his cunning adviser, Kautilya Chanakya, he raised an army, marched on the Nanda capital, and started a civil war. In 322 BCE, he grabbed the throne and threw out the Nandas for good, and began his own Mauryan Empire.

NORTHERN CONQUERING

Chandragupta expanded his territory by attacking the Macedonian General Seleucus and grabbing some of modern-day Pakistan and Afghanistan. Eventually, Chandragupta and Seleucus agreed on the borders of their neighboring territories, and Chandragupta gained the Punjab in northern India in return for 500 war elephants.

HARDOMETER

CUNNING: 6
COURAGE: 7
SURVIVAL SKILLS: 4
RUTHLESSNESS: 8

SOUTHERN CONQUERING

Chandragupta ruled from his vast capital city at Pataliputra. He kept an army of 60,000 foot soldiers, 30,000 cavalry, and 9,000 war elephants. Now that he had most of northern India as well as a lot of other territory in his clutches, he marched his army south, and succeeded in conquering more land. He ended up with most of northern and central India, though he was irritated that the kingdom of Kalinga in the east was not conquered as part of his empire.

ENORMOUS EMPIRE

Chandragupta gave up being emperor in 298 BCE, and passed the government of his Mauryan Empire on to his son. His grandson, Ashoka, expanded the empire to its largest extent. It covered almost the whole of India, and a lot of what is now Pakistan, Afghanistan, and Bangladesh, and lasted until 185 BCE. Chandragupta became a follower of the non-violent Jain religion, and is said to have starved himself to death in a cave.

KING KAMEHAMEHA I

King Kamehameha was a fierce warrior king who united and ruled the Hawaiian Islands.

HARD AS NAILS RATING: 8

YOUNG KAMEHAMEHA

Legend has it that when Kamehameha was born around 1758, storms and strange lights in the sky were signs that he would become a great chief. He was trained to fight and navigate, the two most important skills for a hard as nails Hawaiian chief. When he was 14, he overturned the Naha Stone (or so the story goes)—a massive great rock that weighed up to 3.5 tons (3.2 tonnes). It was said that whoever could lift the stone would unite the Hawaiian Islands.

HAWAIIAN FIGHTING

There was a lot of fighting in the Hawaiian Islands. When a king died, it almost always meant a huge fight over who would take control. When Captain Cook arrived in 1779, some Hawaiians thought he was Lono, the god of peace and plenty. Fighting stopped for a while, but once they realized that Cook was just an English explorer and not a god, fighting resumed. By this time, Kamehameha had proved himself a tough warrior. He was at the battle in which Captain Cook was killed.

KING OF HAWAII

Kamehameha's cousin became king of Hawaii when Kamehameha's uncle died in 1782. The two cousins didn't like each other. Five chiefs supported Kamehameha, and, after several fights, his cousin was defeated and killed. Kamehameha still had to convince the other Hawaiian chiefs to support him, but in 1791, he became king of Hawaii, having beaten everyone else into submission.

UNITED ISLANDS

Over the next 19 years, Kamehameha fought all the other islands with his fleets of canoes and 10,000 soldiers. He was a ferocious warrior, but he was given a helping hand by new European weapons—his warriors now had muskets and cannons. Eventually, after a lot of fighting, Kamehameha became ruler of all the Hawaiian Islands in 1810.

INDEPENDENT HAWAII

Kamehameha ruled his united Hawaiian Islands skillfully, dealing with the Americans, the English, the Spanish, and the Russians, who all wanted the islands for themselves. He encouraged trade, but kept Hawaii independent. Kamehameha died in 1819. Hawaii became part of the United States in 1898.

HARDOMETER

CUNNING: 8
COURAGE: 9
SURVIVAL SKILLS: 7
RUTHLESSNESS: 8

HATSHEPSUT

Hatshepsut changed the way ancient Egypt was run, and became its first female ruler.

PHANTASTIC PHARAOHS

Pharaohs were powerful kings who ruled Egypt from around 5,000 years ago until 30 BCE, when Cleopatra died. Hatshepsut lived around 3,500 years ago. She was the daughter of the warrior pharaoh Thutmose I, and his wife Ahmose. Hatshepsut became the chief wife of Thutmose II, who was also Thutmose I's son and Hatshepsut's half-brother (the Egyptian royal families often married their own brothers and sisters because it strengthened their claim to the throne). When Hatshepsut's husband/brother died in about 1479 BCE, Hatshepsut didn't have any sons, so Thutmose's son by a different wife became the new pharaoh, Thutmose III.

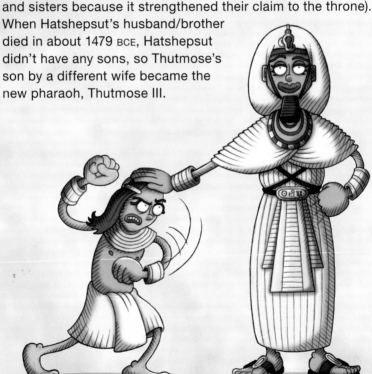

BECOMING PHARAOH

Thutmose III was still a child, so Hatshepsut ruled for him, supposedly just until he was old enough to rule on his own. But, after a few years, Hatshepsut decided she liked being the most important person in the known world. She made sure it stayed that way by having herself crowned pharaoh. This was the first time a woman had ever become pharaoh of Egypt. Even after Thutmose became an adult, Hatshepsut ruled alongside him. Pharaohs were worshiped as gods, and when they died they were believed to take their place among the other Egyptian gods. Hatshepsut did not want to give up her chance to be a god.

WAR AND PEACE

Hatshepsut's reign was peaceful, although she might have taken part in a battle against Nubia, to the south of ancient Egypt. Instead of fighting, she traveled to the land of Punt, which is believed to have been in northeastern Africa. She brought back exotic spices and plants, as well as gold and ebony. She also built impressive and expensive buildings, including her temple at Deir el-Bahri.

REWRITING THE PAST

Hatshepsut died in 1458 BCE and Thutmose III could finally rule on his own. Toward the end of his reign, Thutmose removed Hatshepsut's name from temples and inscriptions, maybe in an attempt to make his own name go down in history as Egypt's greatest ruler, or maybe because he wanted his revenge. Either way, he didn't succeed, and Hatshepsut is still remembered as the first female Egyptian pharaoh.

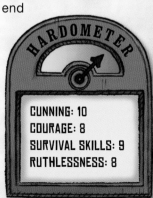

HARDOMETER

CUNNING: 10
COURAGE: 8
SURVIVAL SKILLS: 9
RUTHLESSNESS: 8

NAME THAT MONARCH!

Like Suleiman the Magnificent (page 50) and Frederick the Great (page 34), some kings and queens have been given names that make them sound impressive. Others have nicknames that don't sound so tough. Can you match these monarchs to the right names?

1. Ordono the Wicked ruled Leon in Spain from 958 to 960, taking over from Sancho the . . .

   a) Ugly

   b) Skinny

   c) Fat

   (Hint: No horse could carry him.)

2. Polish ruler Boleslaw IV was nicknamed Boleslaw the . . .

   a) Curly

   b) Hairy

   c) Bald

   (Hint: Women might have envied his hair.)

SULEIMAN THE MAGNIFICENT

28

3. Legendary Viking ruler Ragnar Lodbrok's name translates to . . .

a) Bushy Beard

b) Twirly Moustache

c) Hairy Trousers ·

(Hint: His legs might have gotten very itchy.)

4. Uros V of Serbia was known as Uros the . . .

a) Timid

b) Weak

c) Strong

(Hint: His army could not defend their country.)

5. Peter I of Portugal was known as Peter the . . .

a) Bad-tempered

b) Cruel

c) Hot-head

(Hint: He had two men killed by having their hearts ripped out.)

6. Spanish Queen Joanna the Mad was married to Philip the . . .

a) Sane

b) Handsome

c) Stupid

(Hint: He was famous for his good looks.)

7. Bulgarian Czar Ivaylo was known as the . . .

a) Turnip

b) Cabbage

c) Carrot

(Hint: You might say Ivaylo had layers...)

8. Olaf III of Norway was Olaf the . . .

a) Loud

b) Proud

c) Quiet

(Hint: He was a peaceful man.)

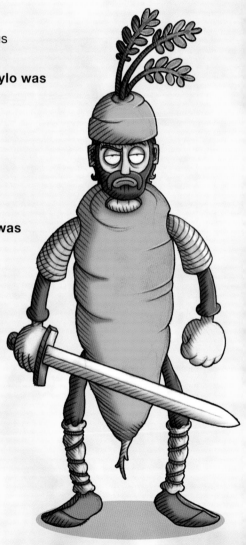

9. **Charlemagne, warrior king of the Franks, had a father known as Pepin the . . .**

   a) Pipsqueak

   b) Tall

   c) Short

   (Hint: He would not have been good at basketball.)

10. **Charles VI of France was nicknamed Charles the . . .**

   a) Mad

   b) Sad

   c) Bad

   (Hint: This guy was crazy!)

Answers: 1 c, 2 a, 3 c, 4 b, 5 b, 6 b, 7 b, 8 c, 9 c, 10 a.

KING SHAKA

Shaka was a hard as nails
Zulu king who did a lot of fighting
and plenty of conquering.

SNAKES AND LEOPARDS

Shaka was born around 1787, the son of a Zulu chief.
However, his parents weren't married, so he wasn't next
in line to become chief when his father died. He grew up
tough. According to legend, when Shaka was 13 he killed
a deadly black mamba snake, and when he was 19 he
killed an attacking leopard. Shaka became a warrior under
chieftain Dingiswayo, chief of the Mthethwa, who were in
charge of the Zulu. Shaka was such a fierce warrior that
Dingiswayo made him commander of his unit.

MURDER AND REVENGE

When Shaka's father died, Shaka's younger brother
became chief of the Zulus. But not for long: Shaka had
him assassinated, and became chief instead—athough
Dingiswayo was still in overall charge. When Dingiswayo
was murdered by a chief called Zwide, Shaka promised
revenge. Zwide escaped his clutches, so Shaka took his
revenge on Zwide's mother by burning
down her house. Zwide and Shaka
continued to be deadly enemies.
In 1825, the two chiefs met in
battle, and Zwide was defeated.

HARDOMETER

CUNNING: 8
COURAGE: 7
SURVIVAL SKILLS: 7
RUTHLESSNESS: 10

CONQUERING

Shaka expanded his lands, either by conquering other groups or by persuading them that they were better off united, with Shaka in charge. His success was partly due to clever new battle tactics and weapons, including a short sword instead of a throwing spear. But he made plenty of enemies, too, especially after his mother died, when he started behaving very oddly . . .

MAKING ENEMIES

Shaka ordered that no crops should be planted and no milk used during the mourning period for his mother. He had thousands of people executed because he thought they weren't grief-stricken enough, and he had cows killed so that their calves would experience losing their mothers.

Among Shaka's enemies were two of his half-brothers, Dingane and Mhlangana. They had probably tried to kill him a couple of times before they finally were successful in 1828.

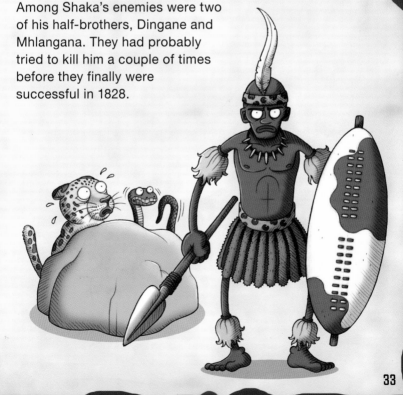

FREDERICK THE GREAT

Frederick the Great did plenty of conquering, making Prussia the most powerful country in Europe.

A BAD BEGINNING

Frederick was born in Berlin, the son of King William I of Prussia (a country that doesn't exist now but which included parts of present-day Germany and surrounding countries). Things didn't begin well for Frederick. His father wanted him to be a tough soldier, but Frederick liked music, art, and studying. The king was so angry that he had his son beaten in public. When he was 18, Frederick ran away, but he was captured. His best friend, who had gone with him, was executed.

WAR WITH AUSTRIA

Frederick became king of Prussia in 1740, when he was 28. In the end, his father would have been pleased. Frederick eventually did become a soldier. One of the first things he did as king was to use his father's large and well-trained army to invade Silesia, a rich Austrian province (which is now part of Poland). This was the start of years of war with Austria, which tried and failed to take Silesia back. Finally, Austria joined up with some powerful friends: France, Russia, Sweden, and Saxony.

THE SEVEN YEARS' WAR

Frederick had England on his side, so more or less the whole of Europe was now at war—and it was all Frederick's fault. He conquered Saxony, invaded Bohemia (which is now part of the Czech Republic), and won battles against the

Austrians, the French, and the Swedes. Finally, in 1763, the alliances fell apart, and Austria made peace with Prussia. Around 180,000 Prussian troops died in the Seven Years' War. After all that fighting, Frederick still hung on to Silesia.

CONQUERING

Frederick managed to almost double the size of Prussia in the end, partly through making agreements with other countries but mostly by invading as the head of a very large army. Everyone in Prussia had to fight. In fact, Frederick had to call in foreign troops, and raise huge taxes to pay them. Frederick died in 1786, having reigned for 46 years. At that time, Prussia was much bigger and more powerful than it had been when he first became king.

HARDOMETER

CUNNING: 7
COURAGE: 7
SURVIVAL SKILLS: 8
RUTHLESSNESS: 8

QUEEN ZENOBIA

Zenobia was a conquering queen who created an empire and rebelled against the ancient Romans.

HARD AS NAILS
RATING: 8.8

QUEEN ZENOBIA

Zenobia was queen of Palmyra, in what is now Syria. Her husband was made governor of the area by the Romans, but he and Zenobia's stepson were both assassinated in 267 CE. There were stories that Zenobia had them both killed so that she could take power for herself. Zenobia's baby son Vaballathus was made king, with Zenobia ruling for him.

TROUBLE WITH THE SASSANIDS

Palmyra was next to the Sassanid Empire, based in what is now Iran. The Sassanids were some of the many people causing trouble for the Romans as their empire expanded into Roman territory. Zenobia led her troops against them and won, gaining more land for Palmyra.

INVASIONS

Zenobia's husband had been happy to rule Palmyra as part of the Roman Empire. But Zenobia wasn't. She led her army in an attack against Egypt. She won, and proclaimed herself queen of Egypt. Then she began a path of destruction across Anatolia (in what is now Turkey), Syria, Palestine, and Lebanon, conquering as she went. She declared herself independent from the Roman Empire as the ruler of her own Palmyrene Empire.

DEFEAT

By Zenobia's time, the Roman Empire had split into two halves. It was weaker than it had been, and faced attacks along some of its borders. But the Roman Emperor Aurelian wasn't about to lose another chunk of his empire. His army defeated Zenobia in battle, then besieged the city of Palmyra.

CAPTURED

Zenobia and her son Vaballathus tried to escape, but were soon captured. The Palmyrenes were forced to surrender (and anyone who didn't was executed), and Zenobia and Vaballathus were taken to Rome. What happened to them in the end is a mystery. Zenobia might have killed herself on the way to Rome, or been executed once she got there. One story says that the emperor took pity on her, and allowed her to live the rest of her life in a comfortable villa in Italy.

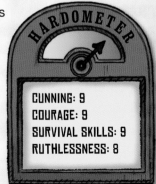

HARDOMETER

CUNNING: 9
COURAGE: 9
SURVIVAL SKILLS: 9
RUTHLESSNESS: 8

WARRIOR KINGS AND QUEENS

Some kings and queens, such as Ferdinand and Isabella of Spain, sent their armies to fight for them. But others, such as Queen Zenobia and Harald Hardrada, liked to get involved themselves. Here are more of the toughest warrior kings and queens of all time.

QUEEN BOUDICA

Possibly the most famous warrior queen of all, Boudica was queen of the British Iceni people in the first century. She stood up to the ancient Romans, defeated Roman troops, and ransacked their capital. She was finally beaten in a battle with the Roman governor of Britain, Suetonius. She killed herself rather than face capture.

WILLIAM THE CONQUEROR

William was the Norman duke who invaded England in 1066, defeated King Harold at the Battle of Hastings, and made himself king of England. He did a lot of looting, burning, and generally made himself very unpopular. He ruled for more than 20 years and passed the crown on to his son.

CHARLEMAGNE

Charlemagne was king of the Franks in the Middle Ages. He was on a mission to convert everyone to Christianity and conquer as many places as possible while he was doing it. He ruthlessly executed 4,500 Saxons at the same time. He conquered much of Europe and founded an empire that lasted nearly 1,000 years.

ATTILA THE HUN

Attila, king of the Huns, commanded some of the most feared warriors in Europe in the 400s CE. He led his rampaging Huns on a path of destruction across the eastern and western halves of the Roman Empire, demanding gold, destroying cities, and setting fires.

ERIC BLOODAXE

Viking warrior King Eric Bloodaxe murdered his brothers so that he would become king of Norway. When Bloodaxe was driven out by a surviving brother, he set sail for the British Isles, raided Scotland, and became king of Northumbria.

QUEEN JUDITH

Judith became queen of a Jewish kingdom in Ethiopia in the 900s. She's supposed to have killed the emperor and put herself in charge. During her 40-year reign, she tried to wipe out all the members of the old ruling family, destroying anything or anyone that stood in her way.

MONTEZUMA II

Montezuma was a conquering Aztec emperor and a great warrior, but he didn't last long after the invading Spanish arrived.

AZTEC CONQUERORS

Montezuma was born around 1466 in Tenochtitlan, the beautiful capital city of the Aztecs that is now Mexico City. The Aztec Empire controlled a lot of Central America and all of what is now Mexico, and ruled five to six million people. Montezuma became a famously terrifying warrior, and helped conquer more land for the Aztecs.

AZTEC EMPEROR

In 1502, Montezuma became the Aztec emperor. He crushed a rebellion the same year, so he used captives from the battle as human sacrifices at his coronation. The Aztecs made a lot of human sacrifices to their gods, and demanded sacrifice victims from the people they had conquered. This was probably why Montezuma had to deal with quite a lot of rebellions while he was emperor. When he wasn't dealing with rebellions, he was conquering, and the Aztec Empire reached its largest size under Montezuma's rule.

HARDOMETER

CUNNING: 7
COURAGE: 8
SURVIVAL SKILLS: 6
RUTHLESSNESS: 9

GOOD GOD!

Mexico had recently been discovered by Europeans. The Spanish conqueror, Hernán Cortés, who had already been conquering in Cuba, wanted to get his hands on the rich Aztec Empire. He contacted some of the many people who were fed up with being ruled by the Aztecs, and ended up with 1,000 warriors on his side from the Tlaxcaltec people, as well as his own troops. The story goes that Montezuma welcomed Cortés into his capital city, thinking he was the god Quetzalcoatl (a prophecy said he would be white-skinned and have a beard). Cortés wasn't so trusting. He assumed the welcome was a trap, and took Montezuma hostage.

MONTEZUMA'S END

Cortés had to leave Tenochtitlan for a battle with a Spanish enemy. While he was away, the Aztecs rebelled. By the time Cortés got back, the Spanish had been driven out of the Aztec capital. Montezuma had been killed in the fighting. Spanish accounts say that Montezuma was killed by the Aztecs, who threw stones at him when the Spanish showed him to his people. Aztec accounts say that he was killed by the Spanish. After his death in 1520, Montezuma's empire fell to the Spanish.

MURAD IV

**Murad was a tough Ottoman
sultan who conquered Baghdad
and executed anyone who opposed him.**

POWER STRUGGLES

When Murad was born in 1612, the Ottoman Empire was already more than 300 years old. Murad was just 11 when he became sultan. His mother and various viziers ruled for him for a few years because he was too young. However, the cavalry and army were really in control, and they executed officials without his consent. In 1632, the army stormed into the palace and executed 16 high officials, plus the grand vizier. Afterward, soldiers rampaged in the streets of Constantinople (modern-day Istanbul), the capital of the Ottoman Empire.

MURAD TAKES CHARGE

Murad was now old enough to rule by himself, and he was pretty furious. He began by executing the soldiers responsible for the executions. Then he banned tobacco and closed coffee houses and wine shops, where plotting might have taken place. Anyone caught or suspected of plotting against his rule was executed. His methods were brutal, but Murad restored law and order and discipline in the army, and the sultan was the supreme leader again.

BASHING BAGHDAD

Earlier in Murad's reign, while he was still a child, the city of Baghdad was captured. In 1638, Murad decided to win it back, leading the army himself and fighting alongside his soldiers. He was famous for his physical strength—it was said he could wrestle several opponents at once and defeat them all. His favorite weapons were a two-handed broadsword weighing 110 pounds (50 kg) and a 132-pound (60 kg) mace. Wielding his enormous weapons, he besieged Baghdad for 40 days, and the city was conquered after a bloody massacre. Murad ended up controlling the land surrounding the city, as well.

DRANK TO DEATH

Murad died in 1640, when he was only 27, probably because he drank too much alcohol. His mentally ill brother Ibrahim took over as sultan after his death, and the Ottoman Empire continued for almost another 300 years.

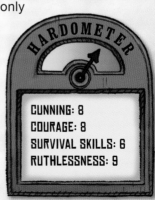

HARDOMETER

CUNNING: 8
COURAGE: 8
SURVIVAL SKILLS: 6
RUTHLESSNESS: 9

NADIR SHAH

HARD AS NAILS RATING: 7

Nadir Shah was born a peasant but became an Iranian ruler. He created an empire and founded a dynasty.

REBEL ARMY

Nadir was born into a Turkish clan in 1688. It was part of the Safavid Empire, which included Iran and parts of Turkey and Georgia. He became a soldier for a local chieftain, then formed his own rebel army. In 1726, he led 5,000 of his followers in support of the Safavid shah, Tahmasp II, who had lost the throne of Iran to an Afghan enemy. Nadir's army completely battered the Afghans, and Tahmasp regained the throne.

NADIR ON THE RAMPAGE

Nadir wasn't very impressed with Tahmasp, and replaced him with Tahmasp's young son—while Nadir ruled for him. He modeled himself on Genghis Khan, the rampaging Mongol conqueror of the 1100s. After a couple of years, Nadir had won back lost territories and he began expanding the empire. His army could cover huge distances with amazing speed, and they attacked just as fast, taking everyone by surprise.

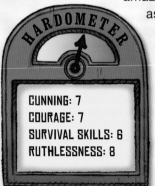

HARDOMETER

CUNNING: 7
COURAGE: 7
SURVIVAL SKILLS: 6
RUTHLESSNESS: 8

INVADING INDIA

In 1736, Nadir put himself on the throne and had the young shah and his family put to death. In 1738, he invaded India, marched on Delhi, killed 30,000 citizens, and stole treasure including the famous Koh-i-Noor diamond.

NADIR KNOCKED OFF

Nadir was a brilliant soldier, but he was not so good at running his newly conquered empire. He made the people of Iran pay enormous taxes, and almost ruined the economy. Eventually, people started to revolt against him. After an assassination attempt, he started to behave very strangely. He had his own son blinded for allegedly plotting against him, then executed anyone who had seen the punishment. Eventually his commanders came to kill him while he slept, but not without a fight—two of them were killed before Nadir was murdered.

ELIZABETH I

Elizabeth was a strong English queen who battled the Spanish armada and ruled for 45 years.

HARD AS NAILS
RATING: 7.3

A DIFFICULT START

Elizabeth was the daughter of Henry VIII and Anne Boleyn. The future queen was only two years old when her mother's head was chopped off on the orders of her father. She wasn't expected to become queen, since she had an older half-brother and half-sister. When her half-brother Edward VI died at age 15, Elizabeth's half-sister Mary became queen. During Mary's reign, Elizabeth was accused of being part of a rebellion and imprisoned in the Tower of London. She was released when Philip II of Spain, Mary's husband, realized that his wife was making herself even more unpopular by keeping Elizabeth in prison. In 1558, Queen Mary I died without having any children. Elizabeth became queen.

TROUBLE WITH MARY

Queen Mary had been a Catholic, and she didn't like Protestants—she had hundreds of them burned at the stake. Elizabeth wanted a Protestant England after her sister's reign, but she didn't burn any Catholics. However, there were Catholic plots against her. One of them may have involved Elizabeth's cousin Mary Queen of Scots, who also had a claim to the English throne. Elizabeth kept Mary in prison for 19 years, then, convinced she was plotting against her, had her executed.

HARDOMETER

CUNNING: 7
COURAGE: 7
SURVIVAL SKILLS: 8
RUTHLESSNESS: 7

SAVED BY THE BEAUTIFUL BRITISH WEATHER!

SPANISH INVADERS

As well as plots against her, Elizabeth also had to contend with threats of invasion. The most alarming one of all was from King Philip II of Spain. Philip had been married to Mary I. He decided get rid of Elizabeth, make England a Catholic country again, and make himself king. He sent a Spanish armada of around 130 ships as an invasion force, but he was thwarted by stormy weather and the English fleet. The threat of invasion remained, and huge piles of cash were spent on defending England, leaving the country in debt when Elizabeth died.

ELIZABETH BOWS OUT

Elizabeth died at age 70, having reigned for almost 45 years. Despite the expensive wars, she was popular throughout her reign—so much so that the date she became queen remained a public holiday for 200 years.

MORE HARD AS NAILS
BRITISH MONARCHS

We've met head-chopping Henry VIII of England and his equally tough daughter, Queen Elizabeth I (pages 10 and 46). But they weren't the only tough British monarchs . . .

RICHARD I

Also known as: Richard the Lionheart
Reign: 1189–1199
Why He's Hard as Nails: Richard joined the Third Crusade, a fight between Christians and Muslims for control of the Holy Land, and in particular the city of Jerusalem in what is now Israel. Although he was a terrifying fighter and had won a lot of battles, Richard returned to England without conquering Jerusalem. But he didn't stay long. He was soon off fighting again, this time in France, where he died besieging a French castle.

MARY I

Also known as: Bloody Mary
Reign: 1553–1558
Why She's Hard as Nails: Mary's father, Henry VIII, had been a Catholic until he divorced Mary's mother, married someone else, and set up the Church of England. We can only imagine that Mary was quite upset by this experience. When she became queen, Mary made England a Catholic country again. She got angry if anyone practiced Protestantism—so angry that she burned hundreds of Protestants at the stake.

EDWARD I

Also known as: Edward Longshanks:
The Hammer of the Scots
Reign: 1272–1307
Why He's Hard as Nails: Edward conquered Wales after
a series of bloody battles. He built forts and castles and
installed English nobles in them to keep the Welsh under
control. He also made his son prince of Wales. Then he
turned his attention to Scotland, where he wasn't so
successful, but caused a lot of battles and bloodshed.
When he finally defeated Scottish rebel William Wallace,
he executed him and had pieces of him put on display
all over Britain.

EDWARD I

SULEIMAN THE MAGNIFICENT

**HARD AS NAILS
RATING: 7**

**Suleiman the Magnificent was
one of the greatest sultans
of the mighty Ottoman Empire.**

OTTOMAN SULTAN

Suleiman became sultan of the Ottoman Empire in 1520.
When his father died, it's likely that Suleiman's brothers
and his uncles on his father's side were all killed, so that
Suleiman wouldn't have any rivals. The empire he inherited
was huge: Suleiman's father, Selim I, had tripled its size
while he was sultan. It included Turkey, Greece, Egypt,
Syria, some of North Africa, and more. Suleiman was now
one of the richest rulers in the world. But he had his own
plans for expansion.

EXPANDING THE EMPIRE

Suleiman's conquests began in 1521, and continued
until he died 45 years later. He rampaged across Europe,
Asia, and Africa, taking what is now Iraq from the Safavid
Empire, rampaging as far west as Vienna, and sailing
across the Mediterranean to capture
all the major ports of North Africa,
as well as the coasts of Italy and
Dalmatia (which is now part
of Croatia). The Ottoman fleet
ruled the sea, commanded by
Suleiman's terrifying grand
admiral, Barbarossa.

HARDOMETER

CUNNING: 7
COURAGE: 7
SURVIVAL SKILLS: 8
RUTHLESSNESS: 6

GOLDEN AGE

With the riches from conquered lands, Suleiman built impressive and expensive public buildings. The empire grew even richer, and arts such as painting, ceramics, and calligraphy flourished. Suleiman's reign became known as a golden age.

SULEIMAN'S LAST BATTLE

In 1566, when he was 72, Suleiman was on his way to Vienna, planning to make it part of the Ottoman Empire as well. He stopped at a castle in Szigetvar, Hungary, with about 100,000 troops. But the castle's commander and his 2,300 men put up a valiant fight. The castle's commander died as the castle was finally lost to the Ottomans. Suleiman died in his tent— maybe of old age, or maybe from outrage that such a small force had cost him so many lives. But by that time, he had an absolutely huge empire that included vast chunks of Europe, Africa, Asia, and the Middle East.

WU ZETIAN

Wu Zetian was a clever, ruthless woman who became the one and only empress of China.

SECOND-CLASS WIFE

When Wu Zetian (also known as Wu Hou) was 14, in 638 CE, she was sent to Emperor Taizong, second emperor of the Tang dynasty. Emperors usually had one wife and many concubines, who were like second-class wives. Wu Zetian became one of them. When the emperor died, Wu Zetian went to live in a Buddhist convent, along with the emperor's other concubines who didn't have children.

JEALOUS EMPRESS

Wu Zetian didn't stay in the convent for long. She was called back to the palace by the new emperor's wife, Empress Wang. She was jealous of the emperor's concubine Consort Xiao, and hoped that having Wu Zetian around might help. It didn't. Wu Zetian became Emperor Gaozong's favorite concubine instead, and that gave her power. She accused Empress Wang and Consort Xiao of witchcraft. They were arrested, then executed.

EMPRESS WU

Emperor Gaozong married Wu Zetian, making her Empress Wu. Any court officials who didn't support her—and there were quite a few—were either sent into exile or executed. Wu Zetian also made sure her own son was named as Gaozong's heir. Emperor Gaozong became sick, and wasn't well enough to rule China. Wu Zetian ruled for him for the last 23 years of his life. She ruled ruthlessly, crushing opponents and rebellions. She also found time to send troops to invade and conquer Korea.

EVICTING EMPERORS

Wu Zetian ruled for Gaozong until he died in 683 CE and her son became emperor, but Wu Zetian was the real power behind the throne. When her son disagreed with her, she sent him into exile and made a different son emperor instead. Finally, she got rid of the second son, too, and took the throne herself. She ruled on her own from 690 to 705 CE. When she was old and sick, a group of her enemies saw their chance. They executed Wu Zetian's friends and made her hand over power to one of her sons. She died in 710 CE, the only woman ever to become empress of China.

HARDOMETER

CUNNING: 8
COURAGE: 8
SURVIVAL SKILLS: 9
RUTHLESSNESS: 9

NEBUCHADNEZZAR II

King Nebuchadnezzar II was an ancient warrior king of Babylon, who made his empire bigger and more impressive than it had ever been.

NABOPOLASSAR AND NEBUCHADNEZZAR

Nebuchadnezzar was the son of the Babylonian King Nabopolassar. The king defeated the Assyrian Empire (with help from his friends the Medes, Persians, Scythians, and Cimmerians), and completely battered the Assyrian capital Nineveh. Then Nabopolassar sent Nebuchadnezzar to make Babylon even bigger by fighting the Egyptian and Assyrian army at the Battle of Carchemish. Nebuchadnezzar won, and the Babylonian Empire got bigger as a result.

KING NEBUCHADNEZZAR

When Nebuchadnezzar became king in 605 BCE, he set out on a path of destruction of his own. He conquered the Cimmerians and Scythians, even though they had helped his father defeat the Assyrian Empire. Instead of conquering the Median Empire, Nebuchadnezzar married the king of Media's daughter. Nebuchadnezzar was kept busy by crushing rebellions, invading Egypt, and capturing Jerusalem.

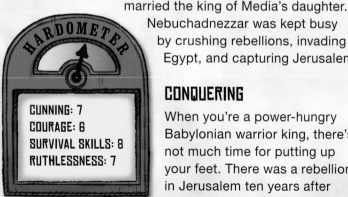

HARDOMETER

CUNNING: 7
COURAGE: 6
SURVIVAL SKILLS: 8
RUTHLESSNESS: 7

CONQUERING

When you're a power-hungry Babylonian warrior king, there's not much time for putting up your feet. There was a rebellion in Jerusalem ten years after

Nebuchadnezzar captured it, and he ended up destroying the city and making many of its citizens leave. Then it was time for more conquering. He laid siege to the city of Tyre in Phoenicia. Thirteen long years later the Phoenicians finally accepted the Babylonians as their overlords. Then it was back to Egypt for another attack.

BUILDING

After all that, Nebuchadnezzar went back to Babylon—but not for a rest. Babylon had been laid to ruins during years of war and rebellions. Nebuchadnezzar restored old temples and other buildings to their former glory. He also built new buildings, city walls, and gates, as well as an impressive stone bridge and underground passage across the Euphrates River. Most famous of all, though there's a chance it might not have been built by Nebuchadnezzar, were the Hanging Gardens of Babylon—one of the Seven Wonders of the Ancient World.

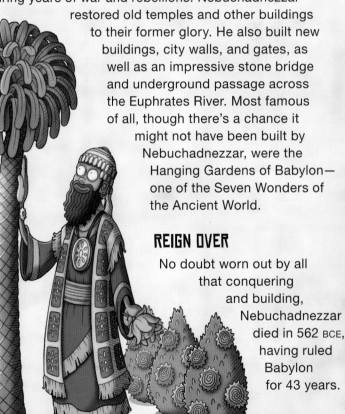

REIGN OVER

No doubt worn out by all that conquering and building, Nebuchadnezzar died in 562 BCE, having ruled Babylon for 43 years.

QUEEN TAMAR OF GEORGIA

HARD AS NAILS
RATING: 7

Queen Tamar was Georgia's first-ever female ruler. She had plans for expansion, and made Georgia the biggest it had ever been.

TROUBLE WITH THE TOFFS

Tamar was born in 1166 CE, the daughter of King George III of Georgia. George named Tamar as his co-ruler. She was 18 when he died and became the sole ruler, and Georgia's first ruling queen. Some of the nobles didn't think she should be running Georgia, and they pushed her around. They got her to marry Prince Yuri, who was a good soldier but otherwise useless to her. Queen Tamar quickly toughened up, put her own supporters in power, and stood up to her enemies. She divorced Yuri and sent him into exile. Then she found a much better husband— David Soslan— who turned out to be a good soldier, too.

EXPANSION PLANS

Now that Tamar was properly in power, she started thinking about expanding Georgia. Abu Bakr of Azerbaijan (which was ruled by Turkey) tried to stop her but Tamar's army, led by her husband David Soslan, defeated him. And Tamar's army didn't stop there. Soon it had conquered enormous parts of Armenia, mainly by invading areas ruled by Turkish and Persian peoples.

BATTLE OF BASIAN

Suleiman II, sultan of Rum, tried to put a stop to the Georgian advance. He camped at Basian (now in northeast Turkey) and sent a strongly-worded message demanding that Tamar surrender to him, and also convert to Islam. If she refused, she would become one of his concubines. The nobleman who read the message was outraged and Tamar sent a curt reply. Then she gave an inspiring speech to her troops, and they battered Suleiman II.

GORGEOUS GEORGIAN EMPIRE

By the end of her reign in 1213, Tamar ruled over an empire at the height of its power. At that time, Georgia stretched from the Black Sea in the west, where she established the Trebizond Empire, to the Caspian Sea in the east. She had also gained more land to the north and much more to the south. As well as plenty of conquering, Tamar had done a lot of praying. After her death, she was made a Christian saint.

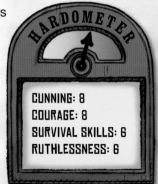

HARDOMETER

CUNNING: 8
COURAGE: 8
SURVIVAL SKILLS: 6
RUTHLESSNESS: 6

HARD AS NAILS
KINGS AND QUEENS TIMELINE

1479 BCE

Hatshepsut became the first female Egyptian pharaoh, ruling alongside her stepson.

883 BCE

Ashurnasirpal II became king of Assyria, and went on to do a lot of conquering.

605 BCE

Nebuchadnezzar II became king of Babylon, expanded his empire, and (probably) built one of the Seven Wonders of the World.

480 BCE

Queen Artemisia of Halicarnassus commanded ships for the Persians in the Battle of Salamis.

340 BCE

Chandragupta, hard as nails founder of the Indian Mauryan Empire, was born.

274 CE

Queen Zenobia of Palmyra, who conquered parts of the Roman Empire, was defeated and captured by the Romans.

690

Wu Zetian became sole ruler of China. She was the only woman in history to become empress of China.

1066

The fierce Viking warrior king, Harald Hardrada was defeated by English King Harold and killed at the Battle of Stamford Bridge.

1213

Queen Tamar died, having conquered a large empire for Georgia. She was later made a Christian saint.

1492

A busy year for King Ferdinand and Queen Isabella, who defeated the Moors, united Spain, and funded Christopher Columbus's expedition to the New World.

1502

Montezuma became the last-ever emperor of the Aztecs, who were defeated by the invading Spanish in 1520.

1509

Eighteen-year-old Henry VIII became king of England. He went on to do plenty of marrying and head-chopping.

1520

Suleiman the Magnificent became sultan of a huge Ottoman Empire, and began a path of conquest to make it even bigger.

1558

Armada-battling Elizabeth I became queen of England.

1623

Murad IV became sultan of the mighty Ottoman Empire, and made it even bigger and more powerful than before.

1624

Nzinga Mbande became queen of the Ndongo in western Africa.

1688

Nadir Shah was born a peasant, but ended up ruling the Iranian Empire.

1740

Conquering monarch Frederick the Great became king of Prussia, which he had doubled in size by the time he died.

1787

Ferocious Zulu King Shaka was born around this date.

1810

Hard as nails Hawaiian King Kamehameha became ruler of all the Hawaiian Islands, after beating or persuading everyone into submission.

LEARNING MORE

BOOKS

Aronin, Miriam. *Merciless Monarchs and Ruthless Royalty* (Shock Zone: Villains). Lerner, 2013.

Ganeri, Anita. *Kings & Queens: The History of the British Monarchy*. Haynes, 2011.

Hansen, Joyce. *African Princess: The Amazing Lives of Africa's Royal Women*. Jump at the Sun, 2004.

EDUCATIONAL WEBSITES

Ancient Egyptian Kings & Queens, Discovering Egypt: **www.discoveringegypt.com/ancient-egyptian-kings-queens**

Monarchs of England, Britain Express: **www.britainexpress.com/History/monarchs.htm**

The Sultans, The Ottomans: **www.theottomans.org/english/family/index.asp**

GLOSSARY

ASSASSINATED Killed for political reasons

BESIEGED Surrounded by enemy forces

CALLIGRAPHY Decorative handwriting or lettering

CHIEFTAIN A powerful leader of a group of people

CIVIL WAR A war between groups of people from the same country or state

CONCUBINE A woman who lives with, and is in a relationship, with a man but who is not his official wife and has a lower status than his wife

CURT Rude and brief when speaking

DIVORCE When a marriage is ended by law

DYNASTY A series of rulers from the same family

EMPIRE A group of states or countries ruled by one leader or state

EXILE Banned from your native country

INSCRIPTION Something written on or cut into a surface

INTERROGATED Questioned thoroughly and forcefully

MACE A heavy club with a spiked metal head

MASSACRE To brutally kill a large number of people

MUSKET A gun with a long barrel

PHARAOHS Leaders of ancient Egypt

PLOTTING Secretly making plans to carry out a scheme

PROTESTANTS A Christian group formed in reaction to the problems they saw in the Roman Catholic Church

PROVINCE An area of land that belongs to a country or empire

RAMMED Roughly crushed or forced

RAMPAGING Behaving in a violent or angry way

REVOLT To rebel

RUTHLESS Showing no pity or kindness to others

SHAH A monarch of Iran

SULTAN A Muslim king

TACTICS Plans or systems

ULCERS Open sores on a body

INDEX